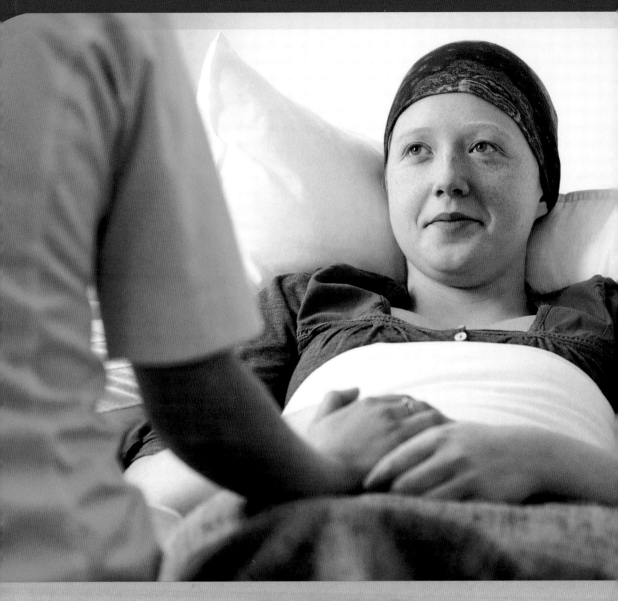

CURING
CANCER

by Meg Marquardt

12 STORY LIBRARY

www.12StoryLibrary.com

Copyright © 2017 by Peterson Publishing Company, North Mankato, MN 56003. All rights reserved. No part of this book may be reproduced or utilized in any form or by any means without written permission from the publisher.

12-Story Library is an imprint of Peterson Publishing Company and Press Room Editions.

Produced for 12-Story Library by Red Line Editorial

Photographs ©: Photographee.eu/Shutterstock Images, cover, 1; Luis M Molina/iStockphoto, 4; ridofranz/iStockphoto, 5; Dean Austin Photography/iStockphoto, 6; vitanovski/iStockphoto, 7, 29; Zeynep Ozyurek/iStockphoto, 8; Paul Vinten/iStockphoto, 9; motorolka/iStockphoto, 11; Alex Raths/iStockphoto, 12, 26; jenjen42/iStockphoto, 13; Eriklam/iStockphoto, 14; Antagain/iStockphoto, 15; Pitris/iStockphoto, 16; BlackJack3D/iStockphoto, 17; xrender/iStockphoto, 18, 28; Science Photo/Shutterstock Images, 19; Dorling Kindersley/Thinkstock, 20; Inok/iStockphoto, 21; Royalty Stock Photo/iStockphoto, 22; Ingram Publishing/iStockphoto, 23; Mark Kostich/iStockphoto, 24; James Steidl/Hemera/Thinkstock, 25; adventtr/iStockphoto, 27

Library of Congress Cataloging-in-Publication Data
Cataloging-in-publication information is on file with the Library of Congress.
978-1-63235-375-7 (hardcover)
978-1-63235-392-4 (paperback)
978-1-62143-516-7 (hosted ebook)

Printed in the United States of America
Mankato, MN
May, 2016

Access free, up-to-date content on this topic plus a full digital version of this book. Scan the QR code on page 31 or use your school's login at 12StoryLibrary.com.

Table of Contents

A Disease Made from Our Own Bodies

The body is made up of trillions of cells. Cells are the building blocks of our bodies. They have many jobs, from helping us think to tasting food. The body must constantly make new blood, bone, and brain cells. However, sometimes things go wrong when new cells are made and cancer starts to grow.

Cancer is a genetic problem that can affect any person at any age. A person's genes hold all the information about how a body should work. Cancer occurs when some part of the genetic code is altered. Harmful forces, such as too much UV light or pesticides, can damage genes. Accidents in copying genes during normal cell growth can also cause cancer. Cancer can occur in

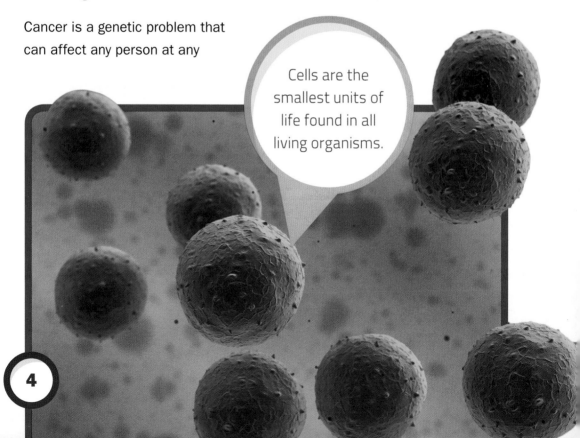

Cells are the smallest units of life found in all living organisms.

The UV lights in tanning beds can lead to skin problems such as skin cancer.

many other ways. Scientists do not know them all yet.

It is difficult to stop cancer once it appears. The many causes of cancer have made it difficult to treat it in some cases. Egyptians as far back as 3000 BCE recorded cancer as a disease with no treatment. Now doctors and scientists are working hard for a cure. From early detection to groundbreaking treatments, modern science is getting closer than ever to beating this terrible disease.

THINK ABOUT IT

Cancer has been around for a long time. Why do you think it is taking so long to find a cure?

1.7 million
Estimated new cases of cancer in the United States in 2016.

- Cancer develops in cells in the body.
- It develops because of harmful forces or genetic problems.
- Cancer has been recognized for centuries, but there is still no cure.
- Scientists are getting closer to finding a cure for cancer.

Treating Cancer Is Challenging

Cancer is hard to cure because no two cancers are entirely similar. Tumors can form in major organs, such as the brain or lungs. Tumors are usually a large grouping of cancer cells. Cancer can also develop in blood and bones. But each cancer is different. A good example is lung cancer. Someone who smokes cigarettes can develop lung cancer. However, lung cancer is sometimes triggered by other harmful chemicals or minerals, such as asbestos. It could also be caused by an inherited gene. Part of what makes cancer so difficult to treat is that it can have many different causes. In fact, some cancers do not have a known cause yet.

Another complication in curing cancer is that it can spread to other parts of the body. This process is called metastasizing. Sometimes cancer cells get into nearby tissue. Sometimes the cells spread through the bloodstream. Removing cancer from the body is a difficult task when it moves around.

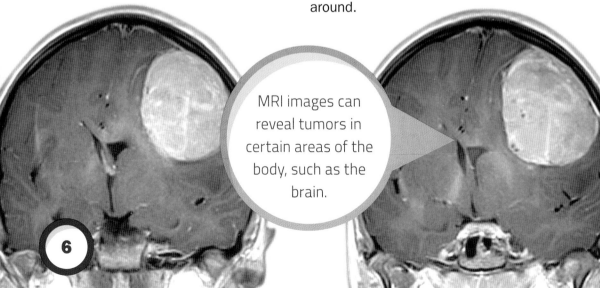

MRI images can reveal tumors in certain areas of the body, such as the brain.

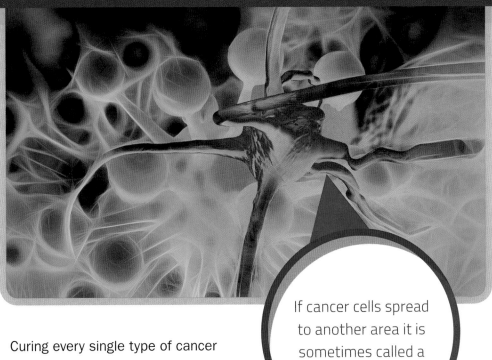

Curing every single type of cancer may seem impossible. But doctors are hard at work creating new treatments that may more effectively fight cancers.

If cancer cells spread to another area it is sometimes called a secondary cancer.

6
Number of mutations needed to turn a normal cell into a cancer cell.

- No two cancers are alike.
- Cancer can have many causes.
- Cancer can get into nearby tissue.
- Cancer is difficult to treat because it can move throughout the body.

CHEMOTHERAPY

The most common cancer treatment is chemotherapy. Chemotherapy involves treatments that use drugs to fight cancer. They can come in the form of pills, shots, or creams. Chemotherapy can also be applied directly to cancer during surgery. Chemotherapy can be effective. However, it can have harsh side effects, such as hair loss and extreme nausea.

New Biopsies Are Better at Spotting Cancer

Like other illnesses, cancer has symptoms. The symptoms vary between types of cancer, but there are some common markers. A patient may have unexplained extreme tiredness, pain, bleeding, or visible lumps under the skin. With these symptoms, a doctor might suspect cancer. The first thing a doctor may do is order a biopsy.

A biopsy is one way to confirm whether a person has cancer before starting treatment. A piece of tissue is taken out of the suspected cancerous area during a biopsy. That tissue is then tested.

Health-care providers use imaging devices to help locate the best place to perform a biopsy. Ultrasounds and x-ray machines are most often used.

Doctors look at and test a biopsy using microscopes and other tools.

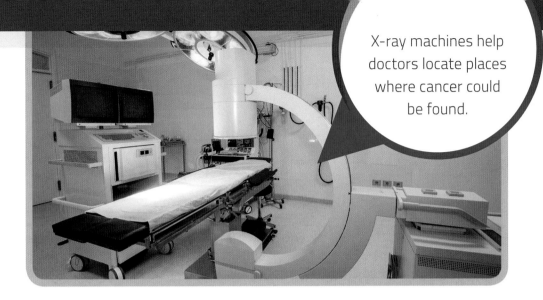

X-ray machines help doctors locate places where cancer could be found.

The images cannot tell a healthy tissue from a cancerous one. But they can help find growths and lumps in unexpected places. These spots are where doctors perform biopsies.

Doctors who specialize in looking for cancer in biopsies are called pathologists. They look for cancer cells and at the amount of cancer cells. This helps determine the stage of the cancer. A stage means how far a cancer has progressed. The higher the stage number, the more dangerous the cancer has become. At stage 0, the cancer is newly formed. By stage 4, it has spread to other parts of the body.

Biopsies carry some risk. Open biopsies are surgeries that require cutting into the affected area.

Newer techniques are not as invasive. These biopsies use very thin needles. The needles draw out a small amount of tissue. Doctors then use microscopes to see whether the tissue is cancerous.

5
Number of stages of cancer.

- Biopsies help diagnose cancer.
- Ultrasounds and x-rays help determine the best place to perform a biopsy.
- A doctor who specializes in biopsies is called a pathologist.
- A biopsy can identify what sort of cancer is in the body and the cancer stage.

Tests Look for Cancer in the Blood

Because cancer can mutate and spread, a biopsy may not be enough to see the entire problem. Not all tumors can be treated in the same way. If the biopsy tested only one tumor, the doctors may not know how to most effectively treat the cancer.

A new diagnostic tool may help researchers understand how complex a cancer is. Liquid biopsies are tests that look for cancer markers in the blood. Cancer markers can be chemicals or genes. Each type of cancer has a different marker. A liquid biopsy requires only a simple blood test rather than surgery. The blood test is less risky for the patient. It is also easier for a doctor or nurse to perform.

Liquid biopsies can also identify cancer cells that have broken away from solid tumors. These cells look physically different from normal cells. They may be too big or too small, or they may have an odd shape. These

FALSE-POSITIVES

Sometimes a cancer test is a false-positive. This is when a test reports that a person has cancer when he or she really does not. An ultrasound may spot something that looks similar to cancer. A biopsy could prove the ultrasound was a false-positive. False-positives can lead to unnecessary treatment. That is why doctors often do multiple diagnostic tests.

Liquid biopsies are a good non-invasive test for doctors to try.

cancer cells or markers could come from any tumor in the body. This means the liquid biopsy does not rely on a biopsy taken from a single location. Because the test is not invasive, it can be done repeatedly. This helps doctors easily find out whether treatments need to change.

14.5 million
Number of US cancer survivors alive today.

- A biopsy sometimes does not see the whole problem of cancer.
- Liquid biopsies look for cancer in the blood.
- Liquid biopsies are less invasive than normal biopsies.
- They can be done many times, which allows doctors to alter treatments.

Ultrasounds May Aid Early Detection

Ultrasounds help doctors locate possible tumor sites. An ultrasound device sends out high-pitched sound waves. The sound waves are used to produce an image called a sonogram. When sound waves strike an object, they reflect back to the ultrasound reader. The ultrasound reader can build a picture of solid objects in the body based on the reflections of the sound waves.

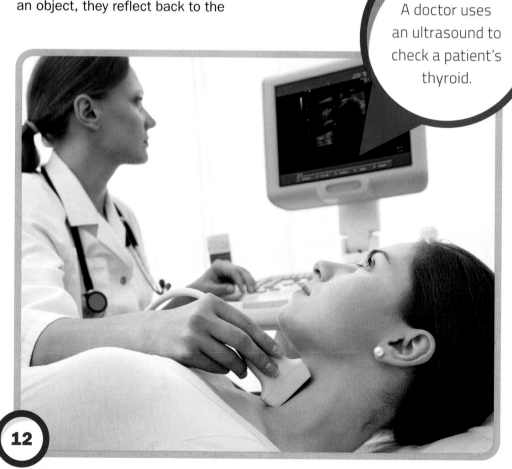

A doctor uses an ultrasound to check a patient's thyroid.

1956

Year an ultrasound was first used for clinical purposes.

- Ultrasounds allow doctors to build a picture of the body's insides.
- Ultrasounds can help identify unexpected masses, which could be tumors.
- Ultrasounds alone cannot be used to diagnose cancer.
- They can be used to help with early detection of certain cancers.

Doctors read the sonogram waves from an ultrasound to determine if there are possible tumors.

An unexpected solid mass in the body could be a tumor.

Ultrasounds are not often used on their own for diagnosis. They may find a mass, but they cannot tell

THINK ABOUT IT

Do some research. What other types of diagnostic tools are available for cancer detection?

what it is made of. Ultrasounds might also be able to tell whether a lump is solid like a tumor or full of fluid like a cyst. This reading depends on how the sonogram waves reflect. But an ultrasound cannot tell whether a mass is cancer.

Ultrasounds are used for early detection. A person with a family history of pancreatic cancer may have an endoscopic ultrasound. An ultrasound device is sent down the throat. This gets the device closer to the pancreas for more precise scans. This scan may help identify the cancer earlier than other tests do. Doctors can then begin treatment before the cancer grows.

Dogs and Devices Sniff Out Cancer

Dogs are known for having superior senses of smell. There have been stories for years that dogs can smell cancer in people. These stories had only been interesting tales until recently. A 2015 study in the United Kingdom put dogs to the test.

In the United Kingdom study, dogs sniffed urine samples. For some cancers, such as kidney and bladder, strange chemicals are released into the urine. Dogs' noses are extremely sensitive. They can detect those chemicals even in extremely small amounts. One dog was able to sniff out cancer chemicals 95 percent of the time.

The dogs were not always correct. They generated many false-positives. A lot of people were recommended for additional tests even though they did not have cancer.

If using real dogs is not reliable, researchers are trying to create electronic devices that can more accurately sniff out cancer. The idea is to build on the information that dogs gather.

Many dogs, especially Labrador retrievers, are known for their sense of smell.

300 million

Number of sensors in a dog's nose compared with six million in a human nose.

- Dogs have such sensitive noses that some can sniff out cancer.
- They are particularly good at smelling chemicals produced by cancer.
- However, dogs generate many false-positives.
- Scientists are hoping to create an electronic device that works even better than a dog's nose.

PIGEONS SPOT BREAST CANCER

Dogs are not the only animals used to help find cancer. A group of pigeons in the United States was trained to identify cancerous tissue taken from a biopsy. The trained birds could pick out a cancer sample 85 percent of the time. Researchers hope to learn something from the pigeons. Researchers might be able to create computer programs that can identify cancer in the same way.

Researchers would then build a "nose-on-a-chip" to put in a sensor. The sensor could be used to detect cancer markers in urine. One day, these sensors might be able to sniff out a wide range of signs.

Pigeons are another animal being trained to spot cancer in humans.

Therapy Targets Cancer at the Molecular Level

Modern doctors and researchers are attempting to find a way to weaken cancer at the smallest level. This treatment is known as molecular therapy. A molecule is a group of atoms. Molecules are part of every cell, cancerous or not. They are responsible for many parts of a cell. Molecules create new proteins. Researchers need to better understand how to control molecules in cancer cells. This understanding will help them stop the cancer from growing or spreading. By targeting specific molecular problems, the treatments could be more effective than chemotherapy.

Doctors are focused on proteins. Proteins are a grouping of molecules. They might be responsible for copying DNA or making up the internal structure of a cell. When a normal cell becomes cancerous, often the proteins in that cell begin to act strangely.

Sometimes cancer cells produce more of a certain protein. Some cancer cells produce a large amount of human epidermal growth factor receptor 2 (HER2) protein. This protein sends out signals. These signals help cancer cells grow at a more rapid

Molecules send out signals to other parts of the cell or body.

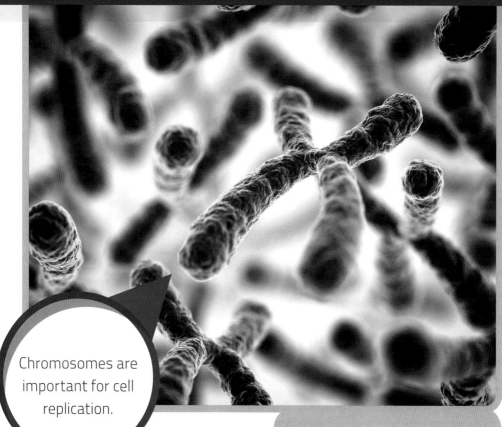

Chromosomes are important for cell replication.

rate than the normal cells around them. Researchers have created drugs that specifically go after HER2. These drugs help slow cancer growth.

Molecular therapy can also be used on abnormal chromosomes. If something goes wrong with a chromosome, strange genes may appear that aid cancer growth. Molecular therapy would fix the chromosome. Or it would stop the chromosome from producing incorrect genes.

1990s
Era when molecular therapy was first used.

- Molecular therapies find specific targets to attack, whereas chemotherapy is more generalized.
- Molecular therapy may focus on proteins or genes.
- Some cancer cells produce large amounts of particular proteins.
- Molecular therapies may try to stop growth or the spread of signals between cancer cells.

Gene Therapy Gets to Cancer's Roots

Many cancers are a genetic problem. Sometimes cancer occurs because of a gene passed down from a parent. Other times, cancer may be caused by a healthy gene that becomes damaged or starts working incorrectly. Treatments that focus on genes seem to be a good starting point. But gene therapy has not always worked well in the past. Researchers hope to change that in the near future.

One idea for gene therapy is inserting a new gene into a cancer cell. This tells cancer cells to stop copying. Another idea is to insert a gene to kill the cancer cell. The gene

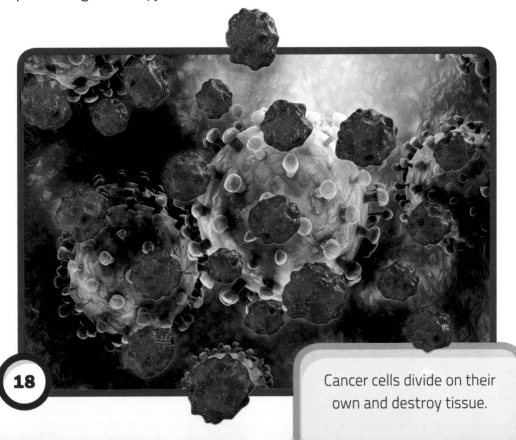

Cancer cells divide on their own and destroy tissue.

THINK ABOUT IT

Some people are worried about altering genetics. Why might people be worried about tampering with genes?

if a gene is kept to the correct cells, the tumor may become resistant. Scientists must figure out a way to keep gene therapy effective and in the right place before the treatment can be commonly used.

Researchers are working on ways to make gene therapy more effective.

can be activated by doctors with a chemical signal or radiation. Once the gene is activated, the cancer cell would kill itself.

However, getting genes into a cell is not always easy. Part of the problem is making sure the gene works in the right cells. The genes must also work for the right amount of time. Major problems could happen if a cancer-killing gene were to get into a non-cancerous cell or tissue. Even

25,000
Number of genes in the human genome.

- Most cancers are genetic problems.
- Gene therapy inserts new genes into cancer cells.
- Gene therapy can cause a cancer cell to kill itself or to stop copying itself.
- Some people worry that gene therapy could affect other healthy cells.

Treatment Chokes Off Tumor Blood Vessels

Tumors need a constant supply of nutrients to help their fast growth. Tumors are full of blood vessels. As the tumor grows, it sends out signals to surrounding blood vessels. These vessels grow new branches. The branches keep the tumor full of nutrients and oxygen. Researchers have been looking for a way to stop the blood vessels from connecting with tumors.

However, doctors cannot create a drug that damages all blood vessels. Strong and healthy blood vessels supply blood to the rest of the body. Most blood vessels are done growing by adulthood. This is good news for cancer research.

Scientists can create a drug that targets blood vessel growth. The drugs may be able to cut off a tumor's nutrient supply in adult cancer patients.

Researchers are also considering blood vessel growth from a different perspective. Blood vessels in a tumor do not work like normal vessels. They tend to have holes. This makes them less useful. Some

A cancerous tumor has its own blood vessels and tissue growth.

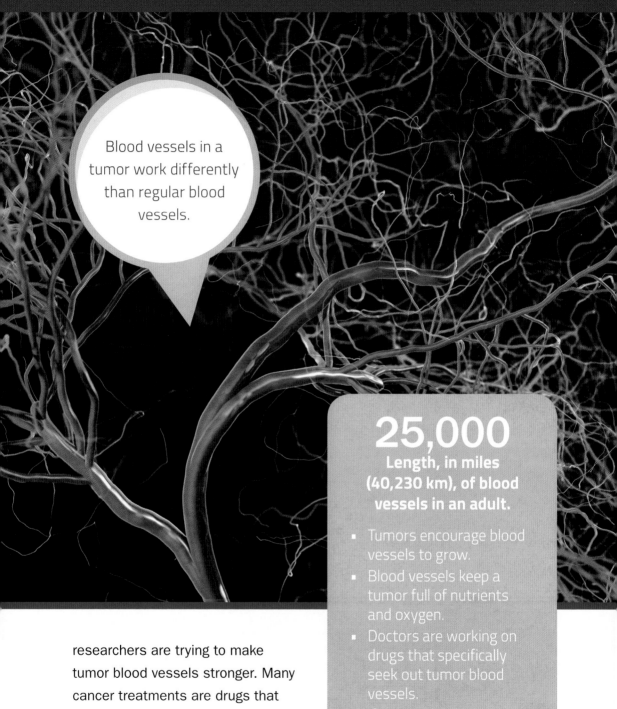

Blood vessels in a tumor work differently than regular blood vessels.

25,000
Length, in miles (40,230 km), of blood vessels in an adult.

- Tumors encourage blood vessels to grow.
- Blood vessels keep a tumor full of nutrients and oxygen.
- Doctors are working on drugs that specifically seek out tumor blood vessels.
- If tumor blood vessels are made to work better, cancer drugs might be more likely to reach the tumor.

researchers are trying to make tumor blood vessels stronger. Many cancer treatments are drugs that travel in the bloodstream. The drugs have a better chance of reaching a tumor if its blood vessels work better.

Immunotherapy Helps the Body Fight Back

The immune system struggles to fight cancer. This is because cancer is made out of the body's own cells. The immune system responds to foreign attackers, such as viruses. But to the immune system, cancer cells look similar to normal cells. Cancer often slips past the body's own defenses.

Molecular therapy and gene therapy might be able to boost the immune system into action. There are two main types of immunotherapy. One teaches the immune system how to better identify cancer. The other inserts human-made elements into the immune system to better arm it for the fight against cancer.

One method of immunotherapy is to remove many T cells from the body. T cells are a main part of the immune system. They are responsible for

Researchers are working to teach T cells to attack cancer cells.

CANCER VACCINES

Vaccines can help the immune system prepare for cancer. A vaccine might help the immune system make antibodies against a virus, such as HPV, that causes cancer. A vaccine may also help if a cancer has already formed. The vaccine may tag a tumor as a problem. It then tells the immune system to attack.

attacking viruses. Once T cells are removed, doctors can insert special genes into them. These genes show the T cells that cancer should be attacked. The T cells are then put back into the body. The gene also allows the T cells to multiply and keep living in the body. This trains the body to fight cancer using its own immune system.

Another method is to insert human-made antibodies. Antibodies are markers on cells that tell the immune system to attack. Cancer cells are tagged with human-made antibodies. The immune system then knows to focus directly on those cancer cells.

3

Number of cancer vaccines that have been approved for prostate and cervical cancer.

- The immune system often does not see cancer.
- Immunotherapy can boost the immune system.
- The immune system can be taught to identify cancer as a problem.
- Researchers have designed ways to add genes to the immune system to make it more responsive to cancer.

Antibodies are large proteins used by the immune system.

Lasers Zap Away Cancer

Lasers might seem like something out of science fiction, but they are useful tools in modern medicine. Lasers are concentrated beams of light. They can be used to kill cancer cells. The beams can be so narrow that surgeons use them as a precise tool to cut away cancerous tissue.

Lasers are used to shrink tumors. Doctors insert a thin cable called a fiber-optic cable into the tumor. The laser light is beamed through the cable. The tip of the cable heats up. It can get so hot that it starts to kill cells. This is not a cure because it does not do anything to treat

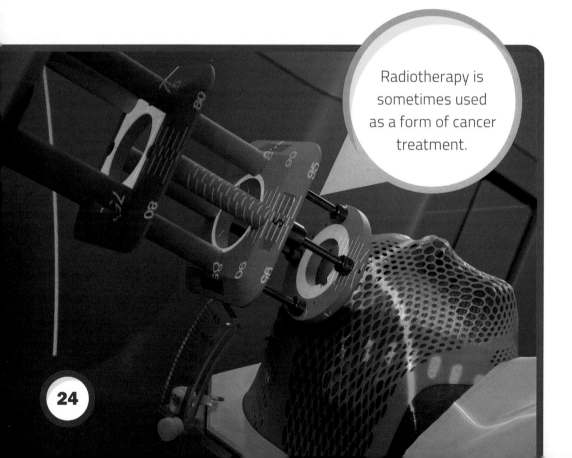

Radiotherapy is sometimes used as a form of cancer treatment.

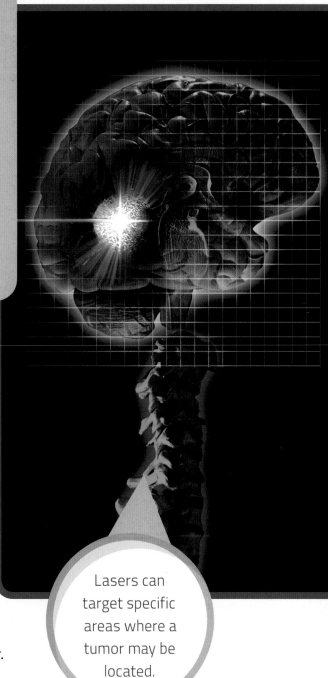

3

Number of types of lasers approved to treat cancer.

- Lasers are used to help burn or cut away cancer.
- Lasers inserted into a tumor grow so hot that they kill cancer cells.
- They can also activate special agents that destroy cells.
- Laser treatments are not cures for cancer.

cancer's cause. But it can shrink a tumor to help other forms of treatment work better.

Researchers also designed a laser treatment that uses tactics similar to those that the immune system uses. The patient takes a drug that has a photosensitizing agent. These agents are sensitive to certain wavelengths of light. Once the agents are in cancer cells, a laser at that wavelength is shined on the tumor. The agents activate and destroy the cells.

Lasers can target specific areas where a tumor may be located.

Human-made Viruses Attack Cancer

Since the 1950s, researchers have been trying to use viruses to help battle cancer. Doctors had noticed for decades that cancer patients who had viruses such as the flu or chicken pox suddenly had fewer cancer symptoms. As soon as the virus went away, though, the cancer came back.

Doctors began looking for a way to make a virus work for the long term. In the beginning, they used viruses found in nature. These included the viruses that cause hepatitis and West Nile disease. But there were many problems. Though the viruses would attack cancer, the immune system would attack the virus. The body would clear the virus and the cancer would come back. Continuous treatment with viruses was not a good option either. The patient suffered side effects. And the more times the body is exposed to a virus, the better the immune system is at fighting it off.

In recent years, researchers have turned to creating their own viruses that might work better than natural ones. In 2015, the very first human-made virus was approved for human use. The virus, T-VEC, directly infects the cancer cells. When the virus destroys a cancer cell, the cell spills out antibodies that tell the immune system to attack the cancer cells. This approach

A doctor works with bacteria from a virus on a growth plate.

THE DANGER OF VIRUSES

One of the major dangers of using naturally occurring viruses for cancer treatment is that the viruses themselves are deadly. For example, in 1949, several patients were purposely given hepatitis, a virus that attacks the liver. Hepatitis had been shown to help slow the growth of certain cancers. Unfortunately, some of the patients who contracted hepatitis died. With the new human-made viruses, scientists hope for less risk.

brings long-term effects. Even if the virus is gone, the immune system now knows to attack cancer. So far, the virus has only been used on a type of skin cancer, melanoma. Researchers hope to develop other viruses to attack different types of cancer.

150

Approximate number of years doctors have suspected viruses might be able to kill cancer.

- Certain viruses seem to slow cancer growth.
- When the virus is gone, the cancer comes back in full force.
- Doctors first used natural viruses.
- Researchers have created a human-made virus, T-VEC, that stays in the body for the long term.

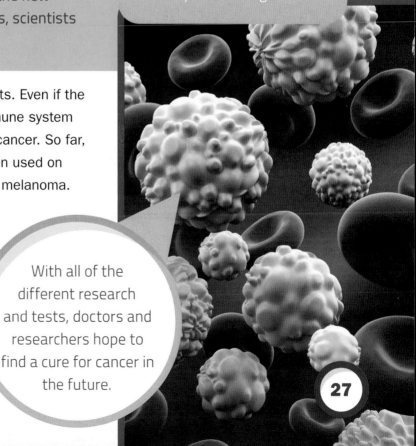

With all of the different research and tests, doctors and researchers hope to find a cure for cancer in the future.

Fact Sheet

- Though cancer is difficult to get rid of, some treatments cause remission. During remission, the cancer cells disappear. Sometimes, remission can last the rest of a person's life. However, sometimes that cancer comes back. Remission is part of why it is difficult to say whether a cancer is ever truly cured.

- The main reason to find a cure is to save people. But cancer is also a major financial burden. In 2010, $125 billion was spent on cancer treatment in the United States alone. Researchers think that in 2020, that number could be as high as $156 billion.

- Though cancer can form in any part of the body, it is more likely to happen in certain locations. For example, the most common types of cancer include breast, prostate, lung, and bladder.

- As cancer treatments become more effective, it is expected that even more people will survive the illness. A total of 14.5 million survivors lived in the United States as of 2014. By 2020, that number is expected to jump to 19 million.

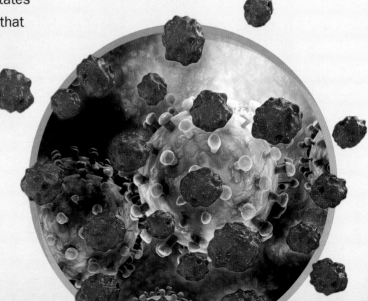

- Though cancer can occur anywhere, the most new cases are in Asia, Africa, and South America.

- According to the World Health Organization, certain conditions and choices could lead to increased risk of cancer deaths. These choices include being overweight, consuming alcohol, and not eating enough fruits and vegetables.

- Early detection is one of the most important parts of effectively treating cancer. This is why women regularly have tests called mammograms. This test looks for breast cancer. Men also are encouraged to have regular exams to screen for prostate cancer. People can also be on the lookout for abnormal moles or spots on the skin that might indicate skin cancer.

Glossary

abnormal
Different than what is normal.

asbestos
A mineral that was used in past building projects and can be harmful if inhaled.

blood vessel
A small tube-like structure that carries blood throughout the body.

cyst
A growth in the body that is filled with liquid.

diagnostic tool
A device that helps identify an illness, such as cancer.

gene
The part of DNA that gives rise to certain characteristics, such as hair or eye color.

genome
A person's complete set of DNA.

invasive
Cutting or putting instruments into the body.

laser
A concentrated beam of light.

mutations
Permanent changes in hereditary materials.

nutrients
Items that provide essential nutrition for living.

pesticides
Chemicals used to kill insects and other animals that damage crops.

tissue
A mass of cells and other biological components.

For More Information

Books

Capaccio, George. *Cancer Treatments*. New York: Marshall Cavendish, 2014.

Forest, Chris. *What You Need to Know about Cancer*. North Mankato, MN: Capstone, 2016.

Squire, Ann O. *Cancer*. New York: Children's Press, 2016.

Visit 12StoryLibrary.com

Scan the code or use your school's login at **12StoryLibrary.com** for recent updates about this topic and a full digital version of this book. Enjoy free access to:

- Digital ebook
- Breaking news updates
- Live content feeds
- Videos, interactive maps, and graphics
- Additional web resources

Note to educators: Visit 12StoryLibrary.com/register to sign up for free premium website access. Enjoy live content plus a full digital version of every 12-Story Library book you own for every student at your school.

Index

About the Author

Meg Marquardt started as a scientist but decided she liked writing about science even more. She enjoys researching physics, geology, and climate science. She lives in Madison, Wisconsin, with her two scientist cats, Lagrange and Doppler.